Poetry Builders

Sophie and Sadie Build a

SONNET

by Amanda StJohn
illustrated by Luanne Marten

Content Consultant
Kris Bigalk
Director of Creative Writing
Normandale Community College

NORWOOD HOUSE PRESS
CHICAGO, ILLINOIS

Norwood House Press
P.O. Box 316598
Chicago, Illinois 60631
For information regarding Norwood House Press,
please visit our website at:
www.norwoodhousepress.com or call 866-565-2900.

Editor: Melissa York
Designer: Becky Daum
Project Management: Red Line Editorial

Library of Congress Cataloging-in-Publication Data
StJohn, Amanda, 1982-
  Sophie and Sadie build a sonnet / by Amanda StJohn ; illustrated by
Luanne Marten ; content consultant, Kris Bigalk.
     p. cm. -- (Poetry builders)
  Includes bibliographical references and index.
  Summary: "Friends Sophie and Sadie learn how to write Sonnets with
the help of their after-school program teacher. Includes creative writing
exercises to assist the reader in writing sonnets"--Provided by publisher.
  ISBN-13: 978-1-59953-440-4 (library ed. : alk. paper)
  ISBN-10: 1-59953-440-1 (library ed. : alk. paper)
  1. Sonnets--Authorship--Juvenile literature. 2.
Sonnets--Authorship--Juvenile fiction. I. Marten, Luanne Voltmer, ill. II.
Bigalk, Kris. III. Title.
  PN1514.S75 2011
  808.1'42--dc22
                              2010043871

Manufactured in the United States of America in North Mankato,
Minnesota.
169N—012011

Words in **black bold** are defined in the glossary.

"Why Writing Poems Makes Me Happy"

I did not always write lots of poems. But I've always loved double Dutch. One day my best friend Sadie came to my double Dutch competition. She really liked the songs we sang while we jumped rope. I told Sadie that I wrote two of them. She said I would love to write poems, too. She was right!

Sadie and I are learning about sonnets in our after-school group. Our teacher, Mr. Hendrick, says sonnet means "little song." A sonnet has 14 lines. Each line has 10 **syllables**.

You have to follow the rules to write a sonnet. Maybe I want to use the word kitty. I might have to say cat instead for it to work. I never know exactly what my poem will say until I finish the whole thing.

Writing poems is fun and surprising! And I think that is what poetry is all about. Don't you?

By Sophie, age 10

"Hey, Sophie!" Sadie shouted. She pulled papers out of her book bag. "Would you like to hear my 'little song'?"

"You mean your sonnet?" Sophie smiled, wiggling her eyebrows. "Of course!"

Sadie stood up and smoothed her shirt. She cleared her throat and read her sonnet.

Would You Like to Pet My Cats?

I have three cats. Each one of them is grand.
Cinnamon Bun chows tons of tuna fish
And takes six-hour naps in our box of sand.
Next up is Slugger. His tail goes "swish, swish."
He sits in the window, watching the birds
But he'll never catch one—doesn't he dream!
Last, meet Bubba Blue, whose mews sound like words
Whenever he begs for a bowl of cream.
I love my cats so soft and so fluffy.
You can come pet them but you have to help—
Brushing them when they start to look scruffy,
Putting food in their bowls before they yelp.

If you're wanting cats, factor this in, too:
No one wants to help clean up kitty poo!

"Eww!" Sophie made a sour face and giggled.

Mr. Hendrick handed the girls juice boxes. "Sadie, your sonnet convinces me that having a pet can be hard work!"

"Thank you!" Sadie said. She punched the little straw into the juice box and took a sip. "Now I want to write a sonnet about another pet I would love to own . . . a purple pony!"

"Purple?" Sophie closed her eyes to imagine it. "That sounds like the most beautiful pony ever!"

"Yeah! I know!" In her excitement, Sadie squeezed her juice box. A fountain of purple juice shot out at Sophie.

Sophie moved out of the way just in time. "Whew, that was close! Hey, can we write the pony sonnet together?"

"Perfect!" Sadie exclaimed. "How should we start?"

Mr. Hendrick waved at Sophie and Sadie. "Come to the whiteboard, girls. Sophie, why don't you number it from 1 to 14."

When Sophie was finished, Sadie added, "Don't forget to leave a little space between number 12 and number 13."

Sophie scrunched her face. "Why?"

"That way we'll remember to save two lines at the end to make our **couplet**," explained Sadie.

"Oh, I remember! The last two lines of a sonnet **rhyme**. Plus, they state a **conclusion**, right?" Sophie beamed at her teacher.

"Exactly, " said Mr. Hendrick. "That is where we tell our readers what to think, feel, or do about our poem."

Sophie turned to her friend, pointing with her marker. "Let's write 12 things we want to say about the pony we love." Sadie picked up her marker and nodded.

1. Well, ever since I can remember, when I was a teensy child

2. I wanted a purple pony of my own really badly.

3. My father always used to say, "purple ponies are still wild beasts."

4. But I am wild, too, just like a pony! So we'd get along great.

5. Purple pony hooves are always made of gold.

6. Purple ponies have neon-pink manes that start glowing at night.

7. Purple ponies sprinkle magic dust with a poof!

8. Ponies love their owners a lot and they always let it show.

9. It's too bad I don't have a pony yet.

10. I dream of one every morning while I eat my oats but

11. my dad says that we need more money and more land

12. because purple ponies need it. He says a rooftop goat would be better.

"Great!" the girls shouted together.

Sadie added, "Sophie, I like when you made the pony's hooves golden!"

"Thank you!" answered Sophie. "I like your part about the magic dust."

Mr. Hendrick read the list. "This is great!
Now, it's time for syllables."

"Syllables?" Sophie bit her lip. "Oh, I
remember! There are 10 syllables in each
line of the sonnet."

"Do you remember how to count them?"
Mr. Hendrick asked.

Sophie frowned a little. "No."

"No," Sadie repeated, clapping once. "No is
one syllable. There are two syllables in
Sa-die," she continued, clapping twice.

"Pur-ple po-ny has four syllables!" Sophie
exclaimed, clapping four times.

"You've got it!" congratulated Mr. Hendrick.

Sadie looked at the pony poem. "We have too many syllables in each line. What can we do to get closer to 10?"

Sophie crossed out some words in line one. Sadie cut words in line two.

1. Well, ever since ~~I can remember, when~~ I was a teensy child
2. I wanted a purple pony ~~of my own really~~ badly.

"Uh oh . . . What do we do about the next line?" Sophie asked. "When I cut out words, it doesn't really make sense!"

3. My father always used to say, "purple ponies are still wild beasts."

Sadie's eyes opened wide. "I've got it! We'll **revise** some things, like this . . ."

3. My dad said, "Purple ponies are still wild."

The girls worked through the entire poem,
erasing some words and adding new ones.
"Now it's time to write our couplet, right?"
said Sadie.

"Uh huh, uh huh, uh huh!" Sophie sang as she pulled her own sonnets out of her book bag. "We can look at one I wrote to get ideas."

Double Dutch

Jump in! Two kids will spin two ropes for you.
While they chant or sing a foot-stomping tune.
You're never alone. You're part of the crew.
It will get anyone's feet moving soon!
Dodging the ropes, you are inside a dream,
Jumping, hopping, skipping—it's all so sweet.
Your heart starts to thump with shouts from your team.
Just do not stop or you will lose the beat!
Heads-up! Here comes something totally new . . .
Don't mess up now when it starts to get fun!
Other jumpers can jump in next to you,
Rhyming and jumping until you are done!

Their moves are so fast—so much to take in!
Watch their feet—you'll learn how to flip and spin.

"Hey, that's a great couplet! In rhymes with spin," exclaimed Sadie.

"I love to rhyme!" beamed Sophie.

"I do, too," said Sadie. "Hey, do and too rhyme, too!"

Both girls giggled. They studied their sonnet on the whiteboard.

"That gives me an idea for our ending." Sophie started scribbling on the board.

Garage Sale, Today!

Well, ever since I was a teensy child,
I wanted a purple pony badly.
My dad said, "Purple ponies are still wild."
So am I, so we'd get along gladly.
My purple pony has a golden hoof.
At night her neon-pink mane starts to glow.
My pony spreads magic dust with a poof.
She loves me bunches and she lets it show.
I have no pony yet to lick my hand
At breakfast while I gobble up my oats,
My dad says, "we need money and more land
To raise purple ponies. How 'bout some goats?"

I guess there is only one thing to do . . .
Sell all of our things and then buy a zoo!

Sadie applauded. "That was so much fun! I'm going to write another. How about you?"

"Bring it on!" Sophie shouted. She clapped—forgetting about her juice box inside her hands. Three little fountains of purple juice splattered on the whiteboard. The surprised girls laughed.

"Aaaaagh! Our purple pony sonnet is being erased by purple rain!" Sophie said.

That gave Sadie an idea for the title of her next sonnet—"Exploding Juice Box!"

You Can Write a Sonnet, too!

The sonnet is very old, and it has many forms. Usually sonnets have 14 lines with 10 syllables in each line. Sonnets end with a couplet that rhymes.

First, find a pencil and a good eraser. You will need to erase often. Number your paper from 1 to 14. Then, think of a subject. For example, you could try to convince your parents to play video games. Write 12 lines that tell us about your subject. Do not worry about syllables yet.

1. Playing video games is the most fun thing to do ever.
2. You can choose a character that has special powers.
3. You can rescue people from big, ugly monsters. You save the day...

After you have notes on all 12 lines, check the syllables. Cut out extra words. Are there words you can change, too?

Finally, write your couplet. In lines 13 and 14, you will write a conclusion. Tell your readers what to think, feel, or do. Remember, it also has 10 syllables per line, and it rhymes.

13. Mom? Dad? Don't let new games scare you away.
14. I promise to help—at least for today!

If you would like an extra challenge, you can make other lines in your sonnet rhyme, too. Look at Sadie's sonnet about her cats. The colors show which lines rhyme.

I have three cats. Each one of them is grand.
Cinnamon Bun chows tons of tuna fish
And takes lengthy naps in our box of sand.
Next up is Slugger. His tail goes "swish, swish."
He sits in the window, watching the birds
But he'll never catch one—doesn't he dream!
Last, meet Bubba Blue, whose mews sound like words
Whenever he begs for a bowl of cream.
I love my cats so soft and so fluffy.
You can come pet them but you have to help—
Brushing them when they start to look scruffy,
Putting food in their bowls before they yelp.

If you're wanting cats, factor this in, too:
No one wants to help clean up kitty poo!

Grand and sand both rhyme. Fish and swish do, too! Take a look at your poem. Choosing your own words, can you make it rhyme?

Glossary

conclusion: the end of the sonnet, used to tell your reader what they should think, feel, or do.

couplet: the last two rhyming lines in a sonnet.

revise: to make changes to your poem.

rhyme: a word that shares the end sounds of another word but has a different beginning—like dust, must, rust, and fussed.

syllables: the bits of sound that make up a word. Each syllable must have a vowel sound. Sometimes the vowel has some consonants with it. *Word* has one syllable. *Syllable* has three—syl-la-ble.

For More Information

Books

Paschen, Elise, ed. *Poetry Speaks to Children*. Naperville, IL: Sourcebooks, 2005.

Prelutsky, Jack. *Pizza, Pigs, and Poetry: How to Write a Poem*. New York: Greenwillow Books, 2008.

Websites

Rhyme Zone
www.rhymezone.com
This website is a rhyming dictionary. Enter any word and it will produce many words that rhyme with it.

Shakespearean Sonnet Basics
shakespeare-online.com/sonnets/sonnetstyle.html
William Shakespeare is the most famous author of sonnets. This website is an in-depth explanation of the form he used.

About the Author

Amanda StJohn is a poet. She is originally from Toledo, Ohio. She teaches students of all ages new ways to communicate.

About the Illustrator

Luanne Marten enjoys creating illustrations on paper, canvas, the computer, and even with her sewing machine! She lives in Kansas City with her husband and is the mother of four grown sons.